In Search of Center

...ramblings on life and sport

In Search of Center

...ramblings on life and sport

Written by Stephen Brown
Foreword by Ethan Zohn
Copyright 2010 Stephen Sinclair Brown

ISBN 978-0-557-69644-4

Dedicated to my amazing family and to all who not only get it, but understand what can be done with it once they understand they have it.

Thank you

Contents

Contents

Foreword

There is a general consensus in the sport of soccer that all goalkeepers are crazy - a different breed of human being. Steve Brown was a goalkeeper. And I think the reason he is having me write this forward is because we have so much in common. Steve is an elite athlete and I'm a former soccer star. Steve has beaten cancer and I'm a recent Survivor. Steve has competed in many ironman triathlons and I have *watched* many ironman triathlons.

It takes a certain type of crazy person to beat cancer and come back to compete at such a high level. But what is most impressive about Steve is what he does after all of the bikes are put away and the goggles are left out to dry. That's when he comes alive. I feel comfortable using the word alive, because that is exactly what he is. He is alive and choosing to get busy living for every single moment.

However, the way in which he lives is very special. Not only is he a husband and father, he lives his life as a selfless leader and teacher. After surviving a cancer experience one would expect a person to focus on himself. Not Steve. He's choosing to live his life to help other people. He has taken the most horrible situation life can deliver and used it to empower himself to go out there and make a difference in the lives' of others. What type of crazy person pulls a stunt like that?

With all of our differences, old or young, man or woman, we all have one thing in common; we're all survivors on this earth for just a short time. But the important questions are not HOW or WHEN will we leave this world, it's WHAT WILL WE DO to make the most of each day and of each crisis while we're here?

I can speak from experience, when you get that cancer diagnosis, you feel alone and panic sets in. All you crave is Survival. You just want to live another day. In that respect, those feelings are very similar to a triathlon where you also experience the panic of not finishing, feeling isolated on the road, and just wanting to make it one more mile. In both situations, once you take away the food and water, and you're tired and hungry, true colors come into focus. All that is left is your strong character, inspirational personality, and the very essence of the human spirit. And these are traits Steve embodies on a daily basis and is able to share with every person he comes into contact with.

You don't have to be Bill Gates or Warren Buffet with fancy titles and huge companies donating tons of money to be able to become a good leader and make a difference. You can just be a little crazy.

As the co-founder of a charity called Grassroot Soccer, I am always looking for skilled natural leaders to work within our sites around the world. Steve embodies everything I look for and seldom find: the ability to lead by quiet example and personal empowerment of the people he is leading. Beyond this, he has—as you know if you have met him—an indefinable quality that draws people to him and opens their minds and hearts to what he has to say.

The world problems that Steve has taken on are enormous—seemingly much larger than any one man or organization could hope to tackle. Watching Steve take on this battle in spite of the odds, I'm reminded not only of his battle with cancer and his ability to finish numerous triathlons, but of the story about a man who plants an apple tree even though he knows that the tree will not give fruit until long after he is gone. Steve's work demonstrates the eternal commitment to laying the cornerstones for buildings we ourselves may never enter.

It's his actions and raw generosity and willingness to help others that make all our lives more manageable.

You know, it's too easy to focus inwardly when you have a setback. And when living the good life, it's too simple to let personal inertia take over and think about nothing but yourself. We all do it at times. The key is, how do we focus on others and how do we rise to the challenges that life brings? How can _you_ make a difference for yourself by making a difference for others? The answer is simple. Just do what that crazy guy Steve Brown does. If we all did that, this world will be a better place.

Ethan Zohn

Preface

I suppose it's important to give folks a little background on how
and why this collection of musings has come to be. The how
part is easy. These are simply a collection of miscellaneous
articles and blog postings on subjects that have spoken loudly
enough to me in my own head to beckon me to spit them back
out for others.

As far as the why part…. I guess writing has always been a
release for me and quite often has even been a part time
profession in a number of ways over the last 10 years. Since
February of 2006, writing took on an even more therapeutic role
for me when I was diagnosed with leukemia. Writing became
another valuable tool in my fight against the disease as I wrote
and blogged about many of the struggles and demons that I
entertained during my diagnosis and treatment. Writing has
always been a coping mechanism for me, and it was even more
so during my treatment.

Today I consider myself extremely lucky and thankful that I am
enjoying such an incredible life; filled with so many gifts and
giving people. My journey over the last several years has
connected me with some amazing people; kindred spirits if you
will and I've learned that so much revolves around the people
that you keep. I don't care how much you think you have in this
world, if your relationships are out of kilter, or if you are not
spending your energy on doing the right thing(s), your flight
plan is way off.

A day doesn't go by that I don't recognize and appreciate all of
the new and wonderful souls that keep finding their way into
my life. This sometimes makes this vast planet seem quite

small, and reminds me that we are all somehow connected to one another by a common thread of humanity.

I certainly don't claim to be a particularly "good" writer. By that I mean, I am not one to sweat the details of perfection. I will never set out with the goal of writing a bestselling anything. I just claim to have an opinion and a little bit of passion. I tell people all the time that I am one of the luckiest people that I know. So I share some of the things that make up that luck and some of the things that keep me awake at night. If by chance something in here resonates with you and you take away a meaningful message, that's great. If not, no worries.

Many of the pieces in this book are simply the result of free streaming consciousness or a message that I really needed to get out there into the universe – for my sake and sometimes for someone else's. And so I decided to pull them together, and toss them back out for all to pick over and ponder.

You will notice a few soccer and goalkeeper references throughout this book. I was a goalkeeper in my previous life and am still passionate about the game. One of the icons of the sport, who I looked up to in my playing days, was a gentleman named Shep Messing. Shep was one of the premiere American soccer players. Shep and I connected later in life and I was touched by the inspirational message from him found in "Messing's Message".

A few years ago, it was Shep Messing who introduced me to another former goalkeeper. It was a very meaningful introduction on many levels and I still have that original email from Shep. It reads as follows: *"...a fellow goalkeeper is now facing a challenge....he's one of the highest quality human beings I've ever met....he went to one of my camps when he was*

10. He was a goalkeeper in college and then played professionally in Zimbabwe before his life took an unusual turn....and I've worked with him and for his charitable causes over the last few years. If you have the time, I know he'd appreciate hearing from a fellow keeper, especially you. In fact, you are just who he needs right now. His name is Ethan Zohn".

The "unusual turn" that Shep referred to was Ethan's lymphoma diagnosis. And that introduction was the beginning of a valued friendship and partnership, as evidenced by Ethan's foreword to this book.

I don't ever want to find myself at the end of my days saying I should have done something or said something to someone. To use the sport analogy, I want to make sure I leave EVERYTHING I have on the field of play, so that when my time here is up, I know I am completely spent. And the people who have been important to me, will all know just how much they meant.

The title "In Search of Center" evolved from an email I received from former professional triathlete, turned respected author and college professor; Scott Tinley who begged the question "How can I find my center if I don't visit my edges?" Those words have stuck with me and they remind me that perhaps writing also gives me an opportunity to both visit the edges, and keep me grounded and true to my own center. In recent years, Tinley has been one of my "go to "people when I am contemplating something that needs validation, or an argument. The respect I had for him as an athlete is nothing compared to how much I admire and respect his insight and more importantly, his brilliant ability to articulate that insight.

x

What lies ahead on the following pages are a few of my thoughts on life, on health, on love, on sport… and on some of the amazing people who have reached and touched me along the way. You will also find a few tributes to remember those who have lost their struggle. I will be the first one to admit, I don't write for any other reasons other than to soothe my soul and clear my head. I sometimes look at writing as good therapy and drug-free medicine all rolled into one.

Enjoy

Messing's Message

All goalkeepers belong to a fraternity of renegades. For ninety minutes you are on the precipice of anger and tranquility. You have to be coiled and ready to strike, with the serenity of a yogi.

That juxtaposition is the greatest mental challenge of every game. You mark your territory and defend it, like a mother bear protecting her den.

At the same time, it is an acutely cerebral undertaking. It's about analyzing, and quickly computing probabilities. You must assimilate everything going on in a game. If you can't see how a game is evolving, you can't make the save.

Steve Brown's fundamental approach towards life was born in this fraternity. Through the challenges he has faced and the obstacles he has overcome, he has taken it to a whole new level.

We are all proud of him.

Shep Messing
Managing Director
Global Sport Group

Rewind

I was a very active kid and involved in every sport that I could sink my teeth into growing up. (And I use the phrase "growing up" in the chronological sense because in so many ways, I feel fortunate that I haven't grown too far up so as to lose touch of the things that matter to you when you are 10 or 12 years of age.) I played three sports through high school and went on to play college and semi professional soccer. I've also never really been sick. I have never had an overnight hospital stay. I have retained all of my God given parts, and have no extra ones. I feel that little bit of health history is an important part of the equation to follow.

I discovered multisport racing in about 1987 and never looked back once I did. I have completed many marathons, triathlons, cycling events, and even many ironman triathlons. I have always felt that I have been blessed with a very charmed and gifted existence. From childhood to today, I have had a great life. Part of that might also have something to do with perspective. See, one of my personality traits is that of adaptability. I can adapt and morph my mindset into whatever it needs to be to make me feel "ok". The downside to that is that "adaptors" might not always have the sense to get out of a burning building because they are too busy being optimistic and trying to make everything "ok". I am learning though that there are certain times in life where you need to jettison your malfunctioning main parachute, and deploy your reserve, rather than spending too much time "fixing" that main chute. OK, perhaps that analogy was a tad off point but accurate nonetheless… somewhat.

At the end of 2005 and in early 2006 I was starting to have trouble swallowing food. My tonsils had become enlarged and I was tripping over them when I ate, swallowed, or even spoke. In early 2006 I was referred to an ear, nose, and throat specialist who wanted to remove my tonsils. I agreed and went through the standard preadmission testing and of course was a little nervous about a tonsillectomy. I had never had any type of surgery at all. But it sounded like it was the right thing to do to fix my problem, or jettison my main chute.

A few days prior to my scheduled surgery, I received a phone call from the surgeon that stopped me dead in my tracks and that nobody ever wants to get. It went something like this, "Mr. Brown we need to put your surgery on hold. Something came back in your blood work that needs a closer look so we are referring you to an oncologist". I was speechless. I really didn't completely comprehend what he was saying, but I did know what an oncologist was. I was pretty certain though that whatever it was would end up being a big mistake, and more of an annoyance than anything else. After hanging up the phone with my surgeon, I immediately called my wife to explain this temporary hold being placed on my procedure.

My wife recommended a top notch oncology practice and I saw the first available doctor in that practice on February 17th, 2006. I went through a battery of tests, biopsies, and scans between February 17th and February 24th 2006. Then on February 24th what was originally supposed to be a tonsillectomy had officially become a leukemia diagnosis.

I ran through the normal course of emotions ranging from denial and disbelief, to anger, and depression. The first question my doctor asked me was whether or not I had been feeling tired. I couldn't tell. I mean probably but let's be real here for a minute… if I got tired after spending 5 hours on my bike, I wasn't thinking leukemia. I was thinking maybe I should take a day off from training. But cancer never entered my mind. Remember… I am the fit and healthy guy.

The hardest part of that diagnosis was going home and sharing the news with the rest of my family. Our family had just gone through a real rough patch. We had lost my father in August of 2005 after spending 3 months in ICU.

My mom also underwent aortic valve replacement and triple bypass surgery in December of 2005 and spent a few months recovering. Our family needed a break in 2006. Nonetheless, I had to sit in my living room and look my kids in the eye and tell them that their invincible ironman triathlete super dad had a blood cancer and needed chemotherapy.

After I ran the gamut of emotions, and had multiple arguments with the voices inside my head, I remembered something very important that I often talk about. I recalled the word "CHOICE". Obviously, I had no choice in the fact that I was just diagnosed. That was the hand that was dealt to me. But I still had choices in how I would handle and respond to my diagnosis and treatment. I made the commitment to send a positive message from the very beginning for everyone else to see and hopefully emulate. I wanted to lead by example. And I wanted to control anything I could in a seemingly uncontrollable situation. I still wanted to be that "athlete". I still wanted to be that super dad.

Since my white blood cell count was elevated off the charts, it was advised that I start chemotherapy treatments right away. I was lucky enough to be able to go to our local hospital for treatment and come back home each day. The treatment protocol was one week of daily treatment followed by three weeks off and this was repeated over four cycles. The cocktails of choice were a combination of a broad spectrum chemo agent called fludara, and a relatively new monoclonal antibody, rituxan.

I was also lucky enough to have my wife with me at every appointment and treatment session. I made the decision to try to be as normal as I could during these treatments. Fitness WAS my normal so I figured that must somehow play a part in my healing. The weeks in between chemo, I worked hard and trained hard to keep my baseline fitness level up so I could knock it down a few rungs during treatment weeks. That was my way of staying somewhat in control.

For me staying in control also meant running home from chemotherapy. On treatment days when I felt strong enough, I would run the short couple of miles back to my house. And the looks on the faces of the chemo nurses were priceless when I would stand up, walk out the door, and run home from treatment. I enjoyed that feeling of defiance. I also used mental imagery on the run home and envisioned cancer cells falling off of my body while I ran and I kicked them into the storm drains on the side of the road. In my role play, the cancer cells were saying "this guy is NUTS. First the chemo and now he's running!" "We can't hang with this dude".

Something seemed to have worked. After two rounds of treatment my doctor referred to me as a "responder". By April I had hit complete remission. By the end of June I was finished all four rounds of initial treatment. In mid July I raced my first sprint distance triathlon as a survivor and on September 30th, just 7 months after being diagnosed, I crossed the finish line of another ironman triathlon (2.4 mile swim, 112 mile bike, 26.2 mile run) with my wife and kids by my side as the announcer and race director renamed me "RemissionMan".

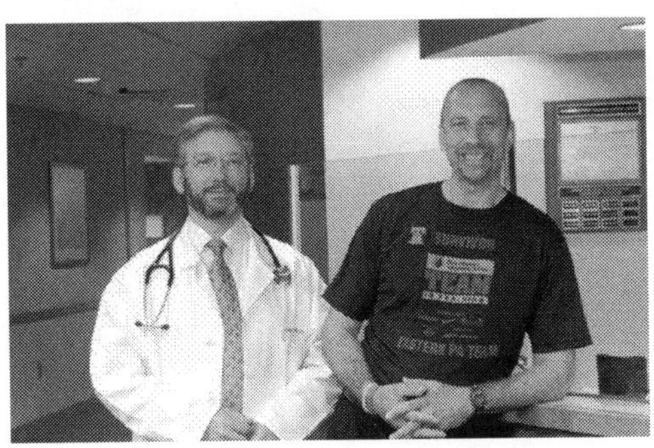

Yes I am proud of all of that but little did I know that the best was yet to come. Within days of being diagnosed, I signed on as an assistant triathlon coach with Team In Training. "TNT" as it is affectionately known is a division of The Leukemia & Lymphoma Society that combines endurance sports training with fundraising in the fight against blood cancers. It was another positive choice that I made. I started working with a group of triathletes who were training for the 2006 Philadelphia Insurance triathlon and it was an immediate connection that has only gotten stronger with each subsequent season. I have been given the opportunity to work alongside an incredible collection of individuals who are all bonded by a common goal; curing blood cancers.

I now completely understand what it means to have "reasons" for a diagnosis. I never really got that before. But there is no doubt in my mind that I was given this to try to work some good from it. I was given this gift to cultivate and reap it into something great. I feel like I am making this leukemia community stronger through my efforts. And we still haven't even scratched the surface.

Why I Do What I do

I have mentioned that I am convinced that there are so many "reasons" for my leukemia diagnosis and more importantly, there are things or reasons that guide me to do the things that I have done as a result of my diagnosis. I may not always know what those reasons are, but the people that I have been able to connect with are too many to mention or even count. I wanted to take a minute and share just a couple of examples of people who have found me or stumbled upon me… or tripped over me as a result of my diagnosis.

When I receive emails like the ones below, I feel like I have a greater purpose and clearer direction. In reading a few of these, maybe you will better understand why I continue to do whatever I can to be a voice and an advocate for this mission.

Steve,

A friend of mine sent me the link to your website, remissionman.com, and I felt the need to reach out to a fellow triathlete/former soccer player/leukemia surviving dad. After browsing your site, I'm beginning to think we're cosmically joined at the hip as the similarities are almost scary. I won't bore you with the details–you've lived them–but I just wanted to enlist you as a valuable member of my own support crew if you're willing. If there's one thing I've learned since I was diagnosed in late 2004, you can never have too many friends. Holler back if you get a moment. Until then, be well. In health and happiness -

Steve,

It's great to read about your story. I was just starting triathlons before my surgery. Someday I'll get back to it. I've gotta take care of a few things first... Keep up the good work!

Steve,

Thank you so much for your story. I too have CLL and am in complete remission. I am less fit and older and your story has inspired me to do something about the "fit" part. Thanks again. Good luck.

Steve,

You are a true inspiration. I am Vince Papale's wife Janet and I relived your struggles. Vince and you are very similar.

Steve,

Hi...

My husband came upon the feature article on you in the January issue of Endurance NEWS. While CLL is probably more common than people realize, we have never seen any articles written about people, athletes like yourself who have had this disease.

I was diagnosed with CLL in 1996 at the age of 47 because of blood work that I had requested just for a good physical only to find my white count was higher than normal. The doctors just kept an eye on it but it never subsided and in 2000 I began therapy and had an autologous bone marrow transplant. I was out of remission after 5 years and again we played the wait and see game. I will be starting chemo in March to try and get back into remission.

I have been biking for many years as well as skiing, doing some weight training and anything else to keep healthy. I think I have succeeded with as much as I am able to control. I have always felt good except during treatment.

I guess the point of writing to you is to try to find out as much as I can about what you did to keep yourself fit as well as your nutrition in general. I am very active and do follow a good diet- except for the love of chocolate, dark of course.

The article actually was refreshing compared to all of the depressing articles on the Internet which I have stopped reading long ago. I want to remain as active and as vibrant as possible not only for myself but for my husband and 6 grandchildren. I really don't have time for setbacks.

Please let me know what you did, what your treatments consisted of, and how your disease progressed.

Steve,

I read your bio on your web site and was very intrigued. I guess I am sending this email because I too have a story. 1 1/2 years ago I quit smoking and drinking and began running. I did my first sprint triathlon (Irongirl) last August and have completed 2 marathons so far. Not only that but in 1995 I was diagnosed with Multiple Sclerosis. I just became a certified fitness trainer as well. I too want to be people's inspiration. I believe if I could do these things anyone can. I want to help people have their own stories to inspire others; I am not sure how to do this, any advice? Thank you

And those are a few reasons why I do what I do. It's all about the people that we meet along the way. Need I say more?

It's Just a (Bigger) Number

Last week I was running at a local high school track and was doing some striders along the yard markers of the nice new artificial turf field. While I was running I was mentally ticking off the yard markers in my head thinking how much longer 10 yards looks on TV watching football than on a mild winter day in the middle of a quiet and empty field.

I started out doing "high knee" or "strider" drills that began at the goal line and went out to the 20 yard line and then jogged back. Then I went out to the 25 and back, etc. I increased these drills in 5 yard increments with each repeat. As I approached the 50 yard mark in bold white letters on the field, a very strange sensation came over me and I suddenly felt that I was no longer measuring distance. Instead, each passing hash mark represented another year gone by. And since 50 is my next milestone birthday, and only a few months away, I was a little apprehensive about hitting that 50 yard marker during my drill.

As my repeats got closer to the 50 I just glared at the mark on the field as I turned back to begin again thinking … "it's coming … soon".

You have to understand something about me and age… I have the soul of a 300 year old, but usually feel like I am somewhere in between 6 and 16. Yes, I have been married for 23 years. Yes, I have 20 and 21 year old daughters and yes I have a 5 month old granddaughter. Yes, I like to play really hard but I like to rest and chill really hard too and take power naps. Not the kind of naps your grandparents used to take. The kind of naps you used to take as a little kid. So, like I said …..I am still somewhere between 6 and 16 years of age with a 300 year old soul that knows how to rationalize why naps are important. The only reason I know that I'm going to be turning 50 is because others remind me of that fact and I can do the math on my driver's license.

Actually, I lied … the real reason that I am aware of my age is because I am required to disclose that info when I register for races. So you tend to become very aware of your age and your opportunity to "age up" into the next age group bracket and compete against kids much older…. Like 51 or 52. You know, the big kids.

The funny thing about the concept of age and the multisport athlete is that it really is just a number. We are all kids. We may feel like 150 year old kids the day after a tough event. But we bounce back like kids too. And the more I think about it, the more I realize that this mindset is not necessarily exclusive to the band of triathletes that I surround myself with.

I think our society as a whole has become much more aware of health and fitness than previous generations have been. When I was a kid, being in your 40's was a half step away from being on social security. Hell, I think I have done more during the decade of my 40's than most people did in their entire lifetime a generation ago.

I have many finisher photos of me crossing the finish lines of races with my kids. I always said that it will be fun to someday be able to do that with grandchildren as well. And now that time has come and we will soon have some pictures that will include three generations.

OK, so take that to the next logical step. Let's just say that my granddaughter has a child in her early 20's. That will put me at about ….. Let's just say a little older than I am now but still racing. Therefore, the very real possibility exists that I will be able to cross a finish line someday with my kids, and their kids, and their kids. Perhaps I am reaching, but that's how I tick and if possibility exists, their only needs to be a bridge to connect possibility with reality. And you are either a bridge builder or you are a stick of dynamite. Don't tell me something can't be done. You will only give me reasons to prove you wrong.

So getting back to those yard markers on the football field that we first started talking about, I stood at the goal line to begin my approach up to that 50 yard line. I started out with slow and deliberate high knee strides to get the real benefit of the drill. This would be it I thought. I needed to hit the 50 to send the right message to the age spirits. I needed to hit the 50, stomp on it, spit on it, flip it the bird, and return back to the start line, proud and triumphant. (yes, I play head games and have discussions with myself all the time while working out).

But no. The 6 year old in me had a different idea. It was a little more difficult, but a hell of a lot more fun and even a little defiant. (Although that 6 year old didn't really get permission for this new plan. He just sort of took off with it as he chuckled to himself.) I hit the 45 yard marker, and then eyed the 50 with an intensity that said "I own you". I picked up a little speed and hit that 50…. Then kept right on going …. 45, 40, 35 …. All the way down to the goal line at the opposite end of the field. When I hit the goal line, I bent down and slapped the line in true high school suicide drill form, turned an about face and sprinted back to my start point. THIS time, when I crossed that 50, I stomped, I spit, I flipped, and I smiled.

It's just a number.

Why Ironman?

People often turn to me for advice or suggestions as they contemplate their first ironman triathlon. Not that I am a blazingly swift triathlete by any stretch of the imagination. But I have been at this game for quite a long time on a number of levels and have completed that distance a number of times. I guess I must have some kind of staying power or possess some longevity gene. This really just translates to the fact that people have been calling me crazy longer than some other people.

People chase the ironman dream for any number of reasons. Many reasons are quite personal and private and even a little complex, while some are as simple as just wanting to be able to say they did it. Ironman is a crazy beast which can often attract crazy beings. The first question that I always ask people is why in the world they would want to put themselves through that? I ask the question rhetorically because I more than anyone know most of the reasons why. Although the reasons may be different from person to person, the underlying allure is not all that complicated to figure out.

But here are my words of both caution and advice…. whatever you choose to do, be humble about it. When you complete an ironman, your initial instinct may be to talk and scream about it from the highest mountain. Be careful how you do that. Savor and reflect appropriately on your accomplishment. Talk about it to your friends, family, and loved ones, but don't misrepresent that elated feeling of accomplishment and self worth into an attitude of "I did an ironman and am therefore so much better than you".

I have seen a number of people get so sucked into the sport and in particular the ironman that their outward displays of pride in their accomplishment can easily be taken as arrogance. A triathlete, check that – ANY athlete - who is true to themselves, is extremely humble about their abilities and their accomplishments. They talk about them when asked but they talk about them graciously.

I have seen a number of people ousted from the real triathlon community because they suddenly started talking about themselves as having attained a greater level of existence or importance because they raced an ironman. Guess what? They didn't. I often see guys raving about their results or broadcasting their workout distances, and trust me, that turns off more people than it impresses.

I don't want to under value the significance of crossing the finish line of an ironman triathlon, or tarnish the quintessential brass ring of the sport. This is huge and you should be very proud of the fact that you even had the courage to attempt the distance. And the redeeming point here is that if you carry yourself right, people know. They just know. You don't have to promote yourself. You can passively wear your accomplishments and achievements like an invisible merit badge and never say a word about yourself. Transcend your accomplishment into actions and live your accomplishment, but don't announce it.

Particularly, pay close attention to how you treat the beginners to the sport, and those race volunteers who work endless hours to make your dreams come true.

Ironman and the triathlon community have enriched my life. The camaraderie and respect among the athletes are like nothing I have ever seen before. The total triathlete is greater than the sum of his or her parts. The triathlete heart, spirit, and the bond that connects us is deeper than that which you will find among swimmers, cyclists, or runners.

So I say, if you really want to race an ironman, make sure you know why you want to do it. Don't race for the medal. Don't race for praise from someone else. Race because you want to dig deep and challenge what's inside. Race because you want to see what you are made of. Race because you have an ounce of doubt that perhaps you can't do it – and want to prove yourself wrong. Race to expand your personal comfort zone. Race to raise money for charity. Race for the right reasons. Be a gentle giant in the triathlon community and use your talents and accomplishments to make a difference … not to make a statement about yourself.

At the end of the day, it's just a race. It's a big race. It's a long race. It's an incredibly rewarding race. But it's just a race. Merely finishing an ironman won't make you a better person. Hell, winning an ironman won't even make you a better person. But if you make the right choices in how you handle yourself and your accomplishments, if you make honorable and meaningful decisions regarding what you do with what you've earned, you can make yourself and those around you better.

And the next time you want to tell someone what your finishing time was, be sure to also tell them how much money you raised for a favorite charity.

Building the Perfect Beast

The genesis of this post is the 1984 album of the same name released by Don Henley. I have always been intrigued by the title and often find myself using it when I talk about putting the pieces of something together. Particularly in multisport training as athletes are constantly trying to strike the perfect balance of several critical components such as training volume, rest, nutrition, equipment, etc. The goal of every athlete is to try to put all of the pieces together that will yield the best result. And with proper planning & preparation, a little luck and perhaps some divine intervention, hopefully you will have built a (near) perfect beast come race day.

But the title speaks to much more than multisport training. "The Beast" concept hit me again the other day when I was responding to a friend's email and I realized that I am constantly in a state of building or creating something or charting a course to somewhere.

I'm not positive I yet know what it is that I am building or where it is that I am going. I'm still not 100% certain of some of my "reasons" for the people that I meet and often don't know what lies ahead but I feel as though I am frequently being guided in one direction or another for a particular reason. And that typically leads me to something or someone who seems to be able to provide the next building block or the next directional turn in my path.

Remember the Shep Messing, Steve Brown, and Ethan Zohn connection that I previously spoke of? Shep did his part in building the beast because he sensed a connection would be valuable for Ethan and I. Shep was right. The number of lives that Ethan has touched is immeasurable and the partnership that Ethan and I have formed as a result is a strong and influential one.

It happened again when I received the following email from a friend:

Hi Steve,
I have a 26 year old young lady who would like to donate volunteer time to work with people who are struggling with cancer. She is in her last semester of college finishing a degree in counseling. I have been working with her and can attest to her character and nature. I would greatly appreciate it if you can help us connect her with the right people/agency to be of service.
Thanks In Advance, Rigs.

Ironically, the above email came from yet ANOTHER former soccer goalkeeper, Bob Rigby, who now works with kids in a local school district and is giving back and paying forward in very big ways. In my playing days, obviously I had no idea how significant the goalie connection would become, although I always did recognize goalies as being a special breed…. with a unique camaraderie.

Of course I was able to connect the woman referenced in the email. And who knows how many lives she may end up touching, or saving. And how many lives those people may touch. It's all part of an ever evolving process. Someday perhaps I will be able to look back on all of this and fully understand how the entire jig saw puzzle fit together. Until that day, I remain very happy to be able to fit pieces in here and there and connect smaller chunks of the puzzle. And I feel very fortunate for the things I have done, the places I have seen, and the people I have met. I know that it is all leading to something very good and very positive; I just can't quite make out the full picture yet. Things are still incomplete and fuzzy. But that's all ok. Maybe even better.

And keeping with the music theme, I guess I find myself "On the Road to Find Out" as Cat Stevens once wrote. And I'm good with that. I'm fine with not knowing all of the answers because I am doing exactly what I remind others to do all of the time. And that is I am enjoying the journey. Don't fret too much about the destination or how fast you get there. But keep your eyes, ears, and heart open so that you can process and enjoy everything along the way.

Appreciating New and Wonderful Souls

I need to first preface this post by giving the appropriate credit where credit is due. "New and Wonderful Souls" were the words used by Vicki Huber-Rudawsky to describe her thoughts on what was a very memorable evening. I liked them… so I borrowed them. The evening went like this…

It isn't everyday that one has an opportunity to meet true greatness face to face. It isn't everyday that one has the chance to sit and listen to an individual who helped change the entire blueprint of women's athletics, and who blazed a trail for millions of young women to follow. It isn't everyday that an icon such as Kathrine Switzer passes through Wilmington Delaware to speak on sports, on believing in yourself, and on how one incident in 1967 facilitated change that will resonate for generations to come. Girls Inc, YMCA of Delaware, Girls on the Run, and Piranha Sports proudly presented Ms. Switzer to a room full of men and women of all ages at the Central YMCA in Wilmington Delaware on October 22nd 2009 as she told her story.

In 1967 Kathrine was a journalism student at Syracuse University with a passion for running. Such a passion, that Switzer proclaimed to all who would listen that she had plans to run the Boston Marathon. The Boston Marathon was second in prestige only to the Olympic Games and was an event in which only men could compete. Or so most people thought for generations past. Studying the marathon rules ever so diligently, Switzer found no documented proof that a woman was prohibited from entering the Boston classic so she took the bold leap and registered for the race under the name of "K.V. Switzer". After all, back then, everyone feared that women were far too weak and fragile to engage in something as physically demanding as the marathon. And we were often told that women should not run any serious distances because….."they would get huge legs, would grow hair on their chest, and wouldn't be able to ever have children".

Kathrine Switzer showed up on race day with her boyfriend Tom, close friend and mentor Arnie Briggs, and a couple of Syracuse cross country runner friends.

What happened next forever changed the framework of women's athletics.

Four miles into the 1967 Boston Marathon, race director Jock Semple pulled up alongside Switzer screaming and demanding that she leave the course, while attempting to physically rip off her race number and remove her. With the help of her entourage, Kathrine held her ground and refused to allow herself to be bullied out of the race for being a female.

Switzer went on to finish that race in 4:20 and 34 other marathons, including winning New York City in 1974 and posting a marathon PR in 1975 of 2:51. But that all still doesn't scratch the surface of the impact that this woman had on the sport and on the world. Switzer went on to create additional opportunities by championing women's events all over the world. She became a voice on the road, in front of the cameras, and in the broadcast booth. She gave a face to the words "belief" and "possibility" and she annihilated the gender barrier.

Following Switzer's talk at the Central Y, several of us were invited to join her for dinner at a nearby Wilmington restaurant. As we wined, dined, and chatted about – everything under the sun, I glanced around and saw a table full of women who were all carrying Switzer's mission and message full steam ahead through the programs of the evening's sponsors. Seated to my left was Villanova running legend and two-time Olympian Vicki Huber-Rudawsky. Seated to my right, was Kathrine Switzer. I shook my head at the profound concept that if "the Boston incident" had played out differently for the woman on my right, the woman on my left would have had an entirely different path in life. As so many women athletes would have.

It really was an evening to appreciate new friendships and "new and wonderful souls", and one that I was honored to be a part of.

Aligning Systems

We went through a training exercise at work not too long ago
called "Aligning Systems". This exercise basically discussed
the importance of having all of the various integrated
components and moving parts of a larger "system" properly
aligned and in sync with one another to be able to operate as
smoothly, efficiently, and effectively as possible. This was an
exercise intended to maximize results in the corporate
workplace but there are huge parallels to be drawn in how we
align each of our own personal systems in order to maximize
our everyday results as we strive towards our real life goals. As
I look at the races that I have on my calendar between now and
the end of November, I find myself in full system alignment
mode. I am at that point where I am taking a lot of inventories
and trying to determine what I have done right, what mistakes I
may have made, and what I need to do to try to tie all of the
pieces together.

The best way to describe this process is that it dissects all of the
things that are required to reach your goal. First, you need to
know your goal – and that is a big problem for many people.
But once you have defined what your mission is, you need to
determine what all of the things, people, or "systems" are that
will assist you in attaining your goal. Once you have the

systems identified you need to examine them and try to determine if each one is operating as efficiently as possible to get the job done.

Picture this analogy… most people have entertainment centers of some kind at home and they may have a number of wires, cables, extension cords, or power strips all plugged in BEHIND the furniture. When you turn on your electronic devices, they all power up so what's the big deal right? Well, I would be willing to bet if you took the time and pulled the furniture away from the wall and examined each cable, wire, and plug and made sure it was connected in the most direct way possible, that you could probably eliminate some unnecessary something and make things a little more efficient. You would also eliminate some clutter.

Ironman Redefined

My father died in August of 2005. He checked into a hospital in June and never left the ICU. I think about him often and wish he was a part of some of the things that have happened in recent years. I really wish he could have met his newest great granddaughter, and attended my daughter's wedding. He loved his kids, grandkids, and great grandkids so much. And man would he have enjoyed the Phillies winning the World Series in 2008. So, I am recycling something I wrote shortly after he passed...

Up until recently, I had a pretty good understanding of what it meant to be an "Ironman". I knew they came in all ages, shapes and sizes but after all was said and done, at the end of the day, I knew an ironman to be someone who crossed the finish line after 2.4 miles of swimming, 112 miles of biking, and 26.2 miles of running. And whether you cross that line in 8:30, or 16:59:59, an ironman is an ironman. This definition changed for me in the summer of 2005.

My dad was 82 years old and never competed in a triathlon. My dad had only a very basic understanding of what a triathlon even is. But he knew that I loved the sport, and for that reason, it interested him. He probably hadn't done any running since his days in WWII. He probably only biked as a kid for transportation and fun. And I'm sure he, like most people, believed that man was not born an amphibious creature and pools were meant for relaxing and cooling off – not for laps. Still, my dad was more of an ironman than I will ever be.

My dad had undergone surgery to remove a tumor in his chest cavity. Surgery itself was successful, but recovery had been a long, rough road. ICU became our base camp for two months.

With each visit to the hospital, I stared at him in amazement. He had his share of ups and downs. Additional procedures were required to handle multiple postoperative complications. Dad did not like hospitals and did not like to be dependent on anyone. So, you can imagine his frustration being in an intensive care unit for so long with all kinds of tubes running in, out, and all around him. He continued to press on. He continued to fight. Even in his times of frailty and weakness, his strength was apparent. He continued to press on even while he was resting. I could feel his determination to get the heck out of that hospital.

Dad fought an amazing fight. But all great fighters and superstars must reach the twilight of their career. It's a part of the cycle. Although dad's will and determination remained as tough as nails until the end, the physical body knew that it was time. And on Friday, August 5, with a room full of family by his side, dad was finally able to get his rest, and his peace, with the dignity that he deserved. He crossed the eternal finish line. He crossed a finish line with far greater rewards and a much bigger celebration than I've ever seen. And I know when it's my turn to cross that same finish line, dad will be there to lead the cheers of the crowd and bring me home.

I learned more about my dad in two months than I had in the 45 years that I'd known him. I have always known him to be strong, yet very caring and sensitive. But it wasn't until recently that I began to fully understand the depths of his strength.

I now have a better understanding of the man who earned a Purple Heart in the War, and the man who always remained loyal and committed to family.

I better understand the man who always did everything within his power to provide a safe and happy existence for his children, grandchildren, and great grandchildren.

I saw a man whose credo was the same as that of the ironman – "To fight…to finish".

Norman Charles Brown, you are missed.

Beautiful Things and New Beginnings

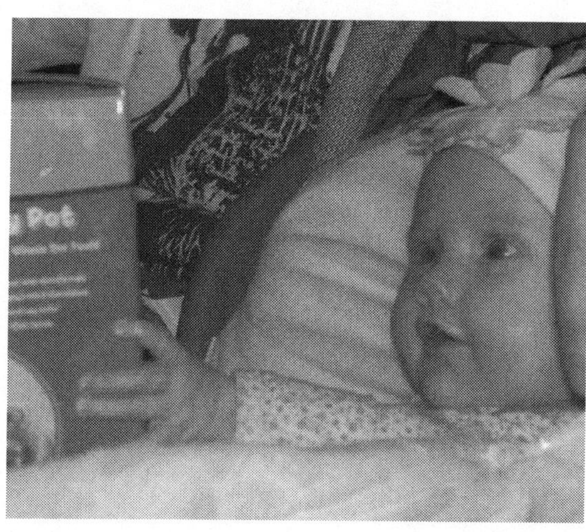

I have always considered my life to be blessed. In fact, you may be tired of hearing me say that by now. If so, oh well. When I look back on my childhood I realize that it was pretty perfect. Flipping through the memories of grade school, high school, college, young adulthood, and parenthood, and seeing where I am today, there is no doubt that I am one of the luckiest guys on the planet. I always thought that I had everything and really didn't feel like I needed or even wanted much else in my life to be happy. Of course we will probably all always want something on some level, but you know what I mean… that stuff would all just be icing on top of a great life.

That perspective changed a little bit for me at 8:52 a.m. on July 29th, 2009. In that instant my daughter gave birth to a baby girl.

Yes, that would make that new baby my granddaughter. I had no idea how special that moment could have been. When I looked at my baby holding a baby that she could call her own everything changed. I feel like she filled a gap that I didn't even know existed. I still don't fully understand the rules of engagement on this new grandfather role. I don't think I am old enough to be one, although I did have some great role models in my father and in my grandfathers. Everyone keeps asking me what my name will be and I have heard a million and a half suggestions but I still have no clue ….

But what I do know is that something incredibly beautiful just entered the world and my life and she has given me a million reasons to want, and to do, and to be even more than I am now.

Brynn Sinclair has raised the bar for me. She has given me new reasons to want to make things better…. Reasons to make HER world better. Hell, she has given me new reasons to make myself a better person. And yeah, I am looking forward to riding my bike to one of her activities in 10 years and hearing one of her friends ask, "Brynn, is THAT guy really your GRANDFATHER"?

I have many pictures of me racing and crossing finish lines with my kids through the years. It has always been my plan to stay healthy and active and keep racing long enough to be able to cross finish lines with my children's children. That goal is now close enough to touch and we have already started talking about which race will be Brynn's first. But now, here is the kicker …. Let's just say for the sake of doing the math, my granddaughter has a baby at the age of 25. That will put me in my mid seventies and I sure as hell plan to still be racing at that tender young age. So does that mean that someday, a four generation finish is in the cards? You gotta believe.

I take pride in the fact that I think I have done a pretty good job at being a good example for my kids. At least I have tried to. I have my faults but I think my heart and my drive have always been in the right place. I'm looking forward to continuing to be that example for another generation.

It amazes me how in one instant, one's world can be expanded by another rung on the ladder.

In the blink of an eye another generation was welcomed in our lives.

And she is loved.

An Abundance of Inspiration

As I approach the midway point of what is shaping up to be a very good and very full racing season, I have found myself in awe of a number of people for a number of different reasons. I volunteered at the Avalon Islandman and Islandkids race in July which are always great events but what stands out most about the weekend is the kid's race. Kids of all ages swim, bike, and run their way to becoming "triathletes".

The expressions on their faces are priceless. Some look horrified, and you just know they can't wait to get finished, others look poised and confident. But at the end of the day, they are all triathletes and are all winners. Races like these can be true cornerstones or defining moments for some kids, and for their parents too for that matter.

Accomplishments such as these are just what some kids need to bolster their self confidence and self esteem. Yes, they are fun and games, but races like these can give kids direction and set them on the right course at a very young age. Unfortunately these events, like others, are not without their share of "stage parents" who put a little too much pressure on their kids to perform. There are great growth and development opportunities in this sport, as long as the parents keep their distance, watch from the sidelines and let the kids be kids.

Another source of inspiration is a guy by the name of John Schultz. I have run into John at 5 or 6 races so far this year. In every race thus far he has won his age group and in a couple of races he has received additional special recognition. John is very distinctive because he always races in red shorts and no shirt and you can pick him out of any crowd. Oh yeah, and John Schultz is 77 years old. Up until this week I didn't even know his name and we simply referred to him as "77 year old guy".

Earlier this week while parking my car on my way to work in downtown Wilmington Delaware, who do you think I saw? You got it – 77 year old guy. I felt compelled to walk up to him and say hello. This idea played out much easier in my head because I practically had to sprint down Delaware Ave. just to catch up to the guy. But I did eventually catch up to him and introduced myself. He actually lives four miles from where I work and was sporting his Sunset Challenge race tee shirt from this past weekend. He was an incredibly nice guy and almost seemed a little shy or embarrassed that I would have remembered him. As we parted ways he said to me with a big smile, "hey there is a local 5k here tonight if you are interested". I can only hope and pray that I am still doing what John is doing at 57 or 67, let alone 77.

Every race has its share of athletes who struggle at the very back of the pack and who seem like they may not even make it to the finish. To see them walking the street you would not picture them participating in a triathlon. But that's the beauty of the sport. It is very accepting of any and all comers. I am far more inspired by the woman who finishes long after everyone else has with a smile on her face and feeling empowered as a result than I am of the elite competitor who smashes a course record.

And then we have the elite athlete who does smash a course
record, but who is so humble that he doesn't like to talk at all
about his own accomplishments. The kind of guy who would
rather give back to others and to the sport than to call himself
elite. I know one guy that fits this description quite well. But I
won't mention him by name as that kind of attention would
only make him feel uncomfortable. He knows who he is and
how I feel about who he is and what he does.

I love long distance training and racing. It's very therapeutic for
me to be on my bike for hours at a time. You tend to figure a lot
of things out during that time and gain valuable perspective
which is useful in all aspects of life.

Words You Long to Hear (and say)

I just wanted to share one small blurb of an email that I received from a friend who was recently diagnosed with leukemia. These are words that every patient lives to be able to say. And everyone else prays to be able to hear:

"As for me, I am on the upswing from my recent bone marrow transplant. My new cells engrafted very quickly which was great. I am still fighting off some of the other side effects that follow a BMT, but am hoping for discharge to home sometime next week. I can't wait to get out of here!"

Comfort Zone Expansion Project

One of the reasons that I became so involved with the sport of triathlon was the fact that it gave me an opportunity to expand my comfort zone dramatically. Not that I had a small one to begin with, but I always felt the need to keep growing mine. I feel it's always a good thing when one can expand their area of comfort, and broaden their horizons and boundaries. I tend to get restless if too much time goes by without pushing the envelope a little bit. When people stagnate in a place that hasn't been challenged, a sense of complacency sets in and you lose your sense of …. something.

When you push yourself beyond your current barriers, (whether they are self imposed or otherwise) you experience a greater sense of accomplishment and reward and with that a greater sense of confidence. Simply put; the greater the risk, the greater the reward. But the beauty is that the sense of improved self confidence carries through to all aspects of life. But if triathlon or sports in general are not your thing, there are still countless ways to expand your comfort zone. I have seen so many people completely turn their lives around simply by taking a leap of faith and trying something a little different, little bold, and a little scary.

So give it a shot. Register for that race. Sign up for that yoga class…. or a painting class. Take music lessons at the age of 50. Skydive. Backpack or bicycle to a place you've always wanted to go. Buy that convertible. Call that long lost friend. Call winners on the toughest court on the playground. Do something that serves as a wakeup call to stimulate you and remind you that you are alive. And should you fail, take a moment and assess what went wrong, make the necessary adjustments ….

AND TRY IT AGAIN.

Three Wise Men

A word of thanks to Ted, Stephen, and Roger

I know I am big on giving thanks and recognizing those people who have made an impact on my life. I have often sung the praises and the importance of the family support that I have always received; whether it was in my athletic endeavors, my leukemia diagnosis, or just living life, I have always had a strong support system. There are three individuals however who have also played a very important role in the person I have become.

I initially wanted to talk about their impact on my athletic life, but looking back, at least two of men also played a key role in helping mold and shape the total person that became Steve Brown. Two of these men were coaches and teachers of mine at Haverford High School in Havertown Pennsylvania. The third is a true fitness expert – no – fitness genius that I had the pleasure of training with for a couple of years in the mid 1980s in Bryn Mawr Pennsylvania.

Education and fitness have always been my hot buttons so it's pretty logical that I feel ties to these three people so many years later.

Ted Keyser coached me in soccer and volleyball at Haverford. Ted, or "TK" as he was known by all, did not look particularly intimidating. He was (is) very slight in stature with a military style buzz hair cut. I knew of Ted before I actually met him. Student athletes either respected the hell out of the man, or detested and rejected everything that he was trying to do. Ted had a brilliant and successful coaching career at Haverford. Haverford boy's volleyball became synonymous with "State Champions". And his soccer teams were a powerhouse year after year.

TK got these results by turning boys into men and forcing them to take ownership for their actions. He ruled with a hard disciplinarian approach. There were some soccer practices that didn't even involve the use of a ball and consisted of nothing but conditioning. But as tough as he was, he was and will always be a good and respectful man. I always wanted to do right by TK. If you kept your nose clean, and gave 110% on and off the field, TK liked you. And TK liking you was always a good thing.

The funny thing is, to this day I think of him often when I am racing and training. I think of the principles and the work ethic that he instilled in us. I think about two words that he used to use all the time – "intestinal fortitude" when things get a little tough. Soccer went on to play a key role for me in college and beyond; thanks to Ted Keyser.

Steve Juenger was my high school basketball coach. Although he was just as successful as Ted Keyser, his approach was from the opposite end of the spectrum. Mr. Juenger was the gentleman coach and really didn't believe in pushing his athletes too far. Instead he was a purest and a perfectionist who believed that shooting 100 foul shots everyday served you much better than doing conditioning drills. It was always a tough transition for those of us who played soccer and basketball.

Since basketball followed soccer in the year, we were all so amped up from so much physical conditioning with TK that it was hard to slow the pace down and shift gears to adapt to Steve Juenger's style of coaching. I even remember asking Mr. Juenger if it would be Ok if we ran some suicide sprints after practice. (Yes, I was a little "off" back then as well). But the thing that I took away from Mr. Juenger was how to be a good person. Sportsmanship and conduct always came first in his book. And that is something else that I try to practice and preach every day.

Steve Juenger was one of the first true ambassadors of good karma in my athletic career. Sadly we lost Mr. Juenger a few years back but his legacy lives large and Haverford has since named their gym after him.

And then we have Roger Schwab. I will have to choose my words wisely because according to Roger, there is no such thing as a fitness "guru", but he is as close as you're going to get without using that term. Roger is the owner and founder of Main Line Health and Fitness, originally known as Main Line Nautilus. I trained at Main Line for a few years in the mid 1980s. Roger's resume is too decorated for me to do it any justice in this brief post. I encourage you to visit their website and read more about their organization and the man behind it.

Roger in a true health and fitness pioneer and was one of the first people to preach the importance of tying "health" and "fitness" together. He hires staff that is committed to the overall health of each and every single member. He was published in the field of women's health and fitness before most other "experts" were deriving any difference between the needs of men and women. It was at Roger's gym that I began to develop a keen interest in exercise physiology and wanted to learn more about the body and how it responded to the stresses of training.

It was Roger's gym that lit the spark in me to go out and receive certifications in personal training and weight room conditioning. Main Line poured a solid foundation of strength and aerobic conditioning principles that I continue to pull from all the time. And when someone asks my opinion on something related to these subjects, I find myself recalling what Roger would say, including one of his classic lines, "You can get strong and fit just by lifting a sack of rocks if you do it the right way". Roger and his buddy Pat Croce gave birth to what became the sports medicine industry.

So, there you have it. I just wanted to give a quick nod to three wise men who I consider very instrumental in the development of – me.

From Where I Sit

I am in a pretty good place; physically, mentally, emotionally, however you would like to measure "good place", I think I am there. My health is now excellent, but my diagnosis left me with a keen awareness of and an appreciation for a lot of things that I may have missed prior to February 24th, 2006.

I was reminded of a lot of things last week when I attended a Cancer Survivors Celebration Day which was held at the local hospital where I had been treated. It is an annual celebration with several speakers including doctors, survivors, and even a comedian. (Last year I was one of the honored survivor speakers.) The odd thing is that the evening started with an informal meet and greet in which tables with refreshments lined the entire chemotherapy and radiation treatment and waiting areas.

Now, you have to try to understand the feeling one gets walking into a chemo treatment center. I always tried to keep things as light as possible. I loved my nurses and when I went through treatment (which, if I did the math right, was 40 sessions over a two year period) I sort of felt as if it was my job to walk in there with as much energy and excitement that I could find. Part of it was done in fun just to drive the nurses a little crazy, and part of it was just my way of dealing. I remember one particular session where I arrived for my treatment before they had opened the doors to start the day. This was never unusual for me as I need to be early for nearly everything that I do. But I was so amped up that morning that the receptionist opened the blind covering their window, and quickly closed it yelling back to the staff, "Steve's here already, who wants him?" And then we all had a laugh once they let me in. Sometimes my energy at 8 a.m. was a little over the top for those just starting their long work day.

So, getting back to my very long winded point … remember … that Cancers Survivors Celebration Day? Yes, so the refreshments lined the treatment and waiting areas. And I was getting such a strange feeling trying to reconcile where we were. Initially I found myself thinking, "Can't we find a better place to do this? Do we have to be so close to the rooms and chairs where the poison is administered to so many people in an effort to kill their respective cancers"?

But the more I thought about it, the more I realized that it was the perfect place to kick off the evening's program. Survivors and their families got the chance to mingle and celebrate in the very area where they had all waged war – and won. It was our own little version of Iwo Jima. We were all Marines and were taking pride in raising our survivor flag in the soil of the treatment center.

The rest of the evening proved to be quite moving and inspiring as well. It is encouraging to see how far cancer remission and cure rates have come over the last few decades. We are winning the war on cancer. There are still many battles yet to come, but we have so many of these things on the run. The work we are doing is helping… all of the donations, and grants, and dedication, and research – this work all saves lives. Don't ever think for a minute that this stuff isn't making a difference.

It is.

And from where I sit, that's a good thing.

An Ironman for an Officer

In January 2002, Upper Darby police officer Dennis McNamara was shot and killed while on duty. McNamara became the first officer killed in the line of duty in the town of Upper Darby. McNamara was a loving father, husband, musician, runner, good cop, and good man.

When I saw the story on the news, I was hit hard. McNamara, was 43 at the time, grew up in Greater Philadelphia, had two children and was an avid fitness enthusiast and runner who spoke often about wanting to someday run a marathon. I saw many similarities between Dennis McNamara and myself and I felt the need to help. I decided to do something that I thought Dennis might have appreciated while helping out the family. I immediately reached out to a couple of buddies in the police department and to McNamara's family and pitched my plan. It was my goal to race Ironman USA Lake Placid in July of 2002 and use my participation in the event to raise awareness of the tragic McNamara shooting, and raise funds for the family. (Ironman = 2.4 mile swim, 112 mile bike, and 26.2 mile run).

I contacted the race management team at Ironman to request that I be assigned a specific bib number: Officer McNamara's badge number 121. The race officials were very open and receptive to the idea, as was the entire Upper Darby Police force who provided me with UDPD workout clothes, and an open invitation to train in their gym facility at the station. The project gathered a lot of steam and publicity and I received well wishes from police officers, and even the widows of officers from all around the country and as far away as Canada.

The race itself proved to be very challenging, as ironman usually does. Harsh rains and flooding made this one particularly tough. But Dennis McNamara was tough, and I hoped to be too that day. It poured rain off and on most of the race. At times my running shoes felt like 20 pound sand bags strapped to my feet. It was a long and tiring day, but I got through it. And all of the pain and rained soaked discomfort disappeared as I crossed the street and approached the Olympic speed skating oval which serves as the race's finish line.

Standing there in the pouring rain, awaiting my arrival, were two Lake Placid police officers. These men were total strangers to me. I glanced up and through the rain saw them huddled together and talking. As I drew closer I heard one say, "Yes, that's him …. Number 121 …. That's the guy for McNamara from Philly". With that, both men stood at attention, saluted me, and thanked me for what I had done. The emotion of the race, the cause, and the site of the Lake Placid cops took me over and I completely lost it.

As if that wasn't enough, as I entered the Oval, there stood my own two daughters ready to grab my hand and run me home across the finish line as they had in races past and in races yet to come. It was a good day.

Shorty after the race, I still wasn't completely satisfied. I needed to do something else. Given the fact that Dennis McNamara was a musician, I wrote a song from the perspective of a 10 year old that lost her dad. I recruited my long time musician buddy Scott McClatchy and told him that I wanted to do something with the song and he took it from there.

Scott made a couple of calls and booked a studio in NYC and the talented producer M. Hans Liebert graciously donated his time, musicians, and resources. When we recorded the song, we did nothing with it other than present it to Diane McNamara in honor and respect for her fallen hero.

It's Got to be Fun

I know I always talk about swim, bike, and run racing and training and how much I love it. And these things really are extremely important to me. But I may have failed to properly convey an important point and I want to be clear on something.

I am not one of those guys that is so type A that I obsess about my race times or finishes. Yes, I have goals, as everyone should. But I don't live and die by my results. I am not one of those guys that gets so wrapped up into training for something that real life becomes an obstacle to their goal.

Enjoying life IS the real goal and the rest of this stuff should only compliment that. It needs to all tie together and none of it should fight for sole possession of you. If your chocolate becomes a stressor, then you need to rethink how you look at your chocolate, or even find a different one.

Sometimes I think many of us have a tendency to get a little too wrapped up in racing and training and we forget that this stuff is supposed to be fun. In a time of advanced training tools and techniques, faster, lighter and better…. everything, it's easy to get so focused on technology and performance that we forget to make sure the experiences are enjoyable. I know many people who won't even get in the saddle unless it's going to be a ride of at least 20 miles. Anything less is "just not worth it" to some.

Every once in a while make it a point to get back to basics by keeping it simple enough to be able to appreciate what's going on around you. Ride your bike like you did when you were 12 years old. (With a helmet of course and without a rider on the handlebars) Run a few errands on an old beat up bike. Ride to a lake with a good book (preferable NOT a training guide) and hang out for a little while. Or, leave the watch and heart rate monitor at home and run to the local convenience store with a backpack to pick up a few essentials. If you have kids, ride or run to their weekend soccer game. Ride the boardwalk of your favorite seashore at 8 miles per hour just so you can enjoy the scenery. Or run barefoot on the beach at sunrise.

These are all ways that although they won't etch a lot of miles in the training log, they get you outside, they get you moving and they keep you fresh. These are particularly good on days when you no training motivation and just can't seem to get moving. Rather than take a scratch for the day, do something fun and simple. It will also jump-start your motivation.

Have FUN

Don't Forget Your Chocolate

OK, I don't mean chocolate as in the cocoa product. I mean chocolate in terms of doing something special for yourself that you love and are passionate about that also fills a void, and satisfies a need, or a sweet tooth. I'm talking about whatever it is that you do that is your "go to" thing to keep you emotionally balanced and on track. Everyone needs something.

By now you all know that my chocolate involves some sort of swimming, biking, or running. (And writing, coaching, speaking, working with kids, or mentoring.) These are the things that I need. These are the things that satisfy my sweet tooth. Take them away from me for a brief period of time and a void is left behind that leaves me restless, uneasy, and a little depressed. Take them away from me for an extended period of time and the consequences could be worse.

You can't plod on day after day dealing with all of life's issues without a little chocolate. And it really doesn't matter what form your chocolate takes. Whether you run, bike, rock climb, knit, bird watch, skydive, read, collect something, cook, or whatever …. Go do it.

Enjoy that chocolate.

Never Forgotten

Here is a race report of a different color. Although the race referenced is the 2007 ChesapeakeMan Ultra Distance Triathlon, there is not much race detail in here. This report is an open letter to anyone who has ever lost someone meaningful in their lives. This report is a letter to my dad who we lost in August of 2005. Although never a triathlete, he exemplified the ironman spirit – especially in his final days.

Dear Dad,

Well, I finished another ironman this past weekend. Conditions were pretty brutal but I finished strong – and happy. I reached out to you a few times and knew you were there. Perhaps that is the reason why I didn't feel like I got too beat up during the race – in spite of some very challenging conditions. Although you never got the chance to see me race an ironman, I know how proud you were of my accomplishments. I really wish you saw one. Maybe we can try to bring mom next time, but it's such a long day.

The race itself was quite tough. There were huge swells in the water and harsh winds. Two buoys were blown off course and the entire swim was a challenge. The winds kept up on the bike which added to the adversity. But this IS ironman. It's not supposed to be easy. I had a few moments of wavering self pity. But this is a sport; a hobby. I signed up for this. And the reality of it is, even with the tough conditions, I had the time of my life and can't wait to go back and do it again. I didn't race my fastest time but far from my slowest and I did pretty good actually given the conditions.

I have been wearing your WWII dog tag recently too. In fact we have a couple of cool race pictures of my shirt unzipped and the tag flying. When I am race, my mind wanders. I sometimes think of your war experiences and try to compare and draw parallels on a simplistic level to what you may have gone through in the islands of the South Pacific. Maybe it's stupid to make such a comparison between sport and the real world, but the mind goes funny (and stupid) places during an ironman. I get a finisher's medal – you received the Purple Heart.

You would have been especially proud of this one dad; the support crew was out in full force. I'm a pretty lucky guy to have my wife, 2 daughters, and brother in law, nephew, and college roommate all out on race day cheering, supporting and volunteering. How many people can say that their families helped them with their special needs bags, placed a finisher's medal around their neck, ran with them across the finish line, and filmed video and took pictures along the way? It makes the races so much more special.

I pictured you sitting in the bleachers at the finish. The same way you would sit with mom at baseball games when I was a kid. You were proud then too.

And this particular race – The ChesapeakeMan Ultra Distance Triathlon is very special. Although it's not huge in numbers, it is run by a world class organization that makes each and every athlete and their family members all feel like champions. It is run by a race director whose staff cares more for the spirit and the camaraderie of the event than anywhere else I have ever seen. He works diligently to make sure the athletes and families walk away from the race saying, "Wow that was a very special experience". These are your kind of people, dad.

We stayed at a friend's house near the race so we had the chance to enjoy the day after the race, which, incidentally, yielded perfect weather conditions. We all hung out on Sunday and enjoyed each other's company and the beauty of the Cambridge area.

All in all, it was a great weekend, a great race, a great venue shared by great people. I connected with some good friends and made a few new ones. That's the beauty of this sport. I can't wait to return.

I also go back in next week for some more preventative maintenance chemotherapy for the Leukemia. No worries on that front though. It's purely maintenance and part of the master plan. Plus I get to sit in a recliner for 4 hours and be waited on. It's not a bad deal at all.

Gotta run for now but we'll talk soon. Thanks for helping me notch ironman number 9 into my belt. Oh, and mom is well. She is being taken care of and doing great. Have a great day (I guess they're all great now).

Much love

Slow Down and See More

One of the points that I made while speaking at the pre race pasta dinner at the New Jersey Marathon was how different your scenery and surroundings look when you run down a road versus when you drive a car down that same road.

When you run down a road, even one you are quite familiar with, you notice things for the very first time; a hidden driveway, a screened in porch, a side street, a dog pen, children playing, a couple on a porch swing…. whatever. You SEE things for the first time because you have slowed down to a pace in which you are actually capable of comprehending and understanding what it is that you are seeing. You miss a lot when you fly down a road at 60 MPH.

Well, you miss a lot when you live your life at 60 MPH too. Slow down. Enjoy the road. Wave to the couple on the porch. High-five the kids. And pet the dog. It makes the journey that much sweeter.

The Girl on the Train

This weekend is the Broad Street 10-miler. I am not racing because I am racing the New Jersey Marathon. But Broad Street is one of my all time favorite races to do. I have done this race many times. And I can't let this week get away from me without sharing a short story about the girl on the train. It's just my way of remembering Barb and a reminder that cancer takes good people all the time.

While riding the subway in Philadelphia to the start of the 1995 Broad Street 10-Mile Run, I met a girl. A great race by the way, but this is not a race report. The girl's name was Barb and I sat next to her and her friend on the train. We exchanged pleasantries. The usual stuff…the weather …the race… Barb was new to the area and had a few race logistical questions. When we arrived at Central High School, the start of the race, we parted ways and wished each other good luck. But for some reason every time I turned around, I kept bumping into her. It became a little ironic, almost like we were unable to say goodbye. Then at one point during the actual race, as I glanced around me, I saw her again. Then again. Then again. Finally, at the conclusion of the race we once again said farewell.

Little did I realize at the time that saying goodbye really wasn't necessary at all. Barb and I would continue to bump into one another all over the place for the next decade. And eventually became great friends. We started as "race friends" in that we would exchange emails and try to say hello whenever we were racing the same events. That led to planning some training together with other friends in our extended running and triathlon families. And before you knew it, a friendship was born. Although the foundation was sprung from our common interest in endurance sports, it led to a more meaningful friendship. And we all know how adult friendships can sometimes be. Months could go by and we wouldn't see or hear anything of one another. But we were always only a phone call away and we always had each other as race buds or tri buds or whatever the heck we were.

I would think nothing of calling her or dropping her an email and telling her to get off of her butt and go train. And she would do the same to me, or for me, depending on perspective. Over time I realized what an amazing talent Barb really was. She was one of those people that completely wreak havoc on something once committing to doing it. When she decided to try her hand at triathlon, she showed no mercy on her competition. I remember one ride in particular. It was right after she really caught the tri bug. We were riding down the shore and I thought I would teach her a thing or two. So, I hammered by butt off into a head wind opening up a huge gap between everyone around me. Everyone except Barb. She was practically in my jersey pocket, smiling. Her look almost said, "OK, now what are we going to do?"

Her top overall and age group finishes are too many to mention. And the girl could swim. I was extremely envious of her swimming ability. But that is to be expected given her all-everything swimming resume growing up and in college.

Through Barb, I met some great people. Through my friendship with Barb, I became friendly with people like Dave Greenfield, President and owner of Elite Bicycles and general ambassador of good karma. And Stuart Trager, who when he is not ripping off sub 10 hour IM's, the Dr. is either in surgery, or serving as a walking Atkins testimonial.

Through me, Barb was introduced to my band of tri comrades in the area. That spawned off some wonderful friendships for her. It was cool how our two independent networks of friends and training partners became intertwined into one. But that too is the beauty of the sport of triathlon.

Barb was an Amazon. She was capable of doing anything she set her sights on. She was a testimonial to Nike, the Greek goddess of victory. An amazingly strong and talented woman when she wanted to be, but very human and fallible at the same time. She eventually learned not to take this stuff too seriously.

She knew how to fully enjoy whatever she was doing. And she knew when she needed a break. If she didn't enjoy something, she would take some time off to regenerate, and then return again with an even bigger zest. After taking some time off to reflect and take some personal inventory, Barb was recharged and believed the upcoming season was to be her best yet.

I spoke to Barb around Thanksgiving of that year. I hadn't heard from her for a while and dropped her an email, which led to a phone call. I was sorry to hear that Barb had been suffering from some kind of respiratory something. Maybe it was the flu, maybe pneumonia. She wasn't too sure but her doc was going to run some tests and with some much needed rest, she was expected back on her feet eventually… eventually.

A couple of weeks later, I got the word that things were much more serious than anyone realized. My friend Barb, the athlete, was diagnosed with stage four lung cancer and her long term outlook was not good. I spoke to her again the day before New Year's Eve. She was back in the hospital. Too weak and groggy to say too much, Barb spoke for a minute but then handed the phone to her sister. The conversation was short. But her sister filled in the missing pieces. As I was talking to her sister, my radio was eerily playing Melissa Etheridge as she belted out the chorus "It only hurts when I breathe". The irony in that is physically painful.

Barb's condition continued to worsen over the next few months. She eventually moved back home to Indiana to be with family during her last days. She fought the way she always did. But in mid-March Barb lost her battle.

How was this possible? Never mind, I know damn well how it's possible. It's life. Precious and beautiful one minute, fragile the next and gone before you know it. But as much as we can understand it on an intellectual level, it doesn't help to ease the gut wrenching pain of its reality.

As much as it hurts and as sad as it is, I feel lucky. I feel lucky to have known Barb when she was on top of her game. I feel lucky enough to have been considered a friend and confident when she wasn't. And I feel lucky enough to have been able to talk to her during her last days. I still don't understand it. But I'm thankful for having been a part of her life and she a part of mine.

A Matter of Perspective

Perspective; I use that word all the time. It's all about perspective…it depends on your perspective …keep it all in perspective. Singer songwriter John Gorka has a great song about being a native of New Jersey. He sings about the girls with the high hair and measuring your socio economic status in terms of Jersey Turnpike exits. In the song he also says "If the world were to end tomorrow, I would adjust". How's that for adaptability and perspective? Maybe John Gorka is a triathlete.

At any rate, I often find myself keeping or putting things into "perspective". A few key universal truths help keep my perspective on track. First point … things are rarely as bad as they first appear. I always try to remember that there are many people who are far less fortunate than I. I have a roof over my head, an amazing family, a great network of friends, my health, and I am gainfully employed in the best nation in the world. For all intents and purposes, my life is a fairy tale.

I also try to remember that most issues and problems are typically short term in the grand scheme of things. In most cases, there will be an end. So, the bigger challenge is not in the crises itself, but in how we accept and manage the crises. That is what will determine our degree of happiness. And that is a choice that we all have. We choose to be happy or not by how we relate to what goes on around us. And how do we do that? We do so by keeping things in perspective.

We could choose to throw a gasket over that traffic jam or bad report card. Or we can take a minute and think through how serious the issue really is. Will it matter next year? Is it something that I can control? Do I need to actually DO anything right at this moment? If your answer to those questions is "no", there probably isn't a whole lot that you should be stressing out about.

One of my favorite questions to ask in times of apparent dire straits is "What's the worst that can happen"? Not because I am tempting the devil or evoking any bad karma. I just want to try to determine the severity of the situation. That way I can have multiple back up plans. I hope for, pray for, and expect the best outcome in any situation… but I try to have a plan for the worst case scenario as well. It may not work for everyone, but it works for me. That way, if I get rocked by something, I can move to plan B, hopefully unscathed.

Something to think about the next time you THINK you are having a crises or a meltdown. When looked at in contrast to the big picture, does this stuff really matter?

Remembering Brad

Brad Schoener was a music director in the Upper Darby Pennsylvania school district for 25 years. He lost a 5 year battle with cancer in March but not before having an amazingly positive impact on the lives of countless people of all ages.

Brad was loved everywhere he went and helped mold the future paths of so many children through his passion for music and his ability to  bring out that passion in his students. I was fortunate to have known Brad on a couple of levels and have reflected on a few of my thoughts …

To say that Brad Schoener was loved is an understatement. Brad radiated passion, commitment, dedication, and joy for his kids and music with every fiber of his existence. There was a piece of Brad left behind in everything that he did and he left an imprint on every person that he touched. And he touched thousands upon thousands. He had an aura. You could feel it when he walked into a room with his head held high or took his position in front of one of his bands. You could see it in his smile. You could see it in his pony tail, and you could see it in the funky socks he wore for performances.

When Brad was diagnosed with a rare cancer, we saw a man who looked straight down the barrel of the gun of his cancer. We saw a warrior who ferociously battled an illness tooth and nail with everything that he had. Brad may have taken some hard hits; but he delivered even greater ones. He kicked cancer square in the face and did damage to his opponent … repeatedly.

We saw a man unleash the strength, conviction, and fortitude of a gladiator. When I was diagnosed with leukemia in 2006, Brad and I shared our appreciation for our lives and the people in them. We discussed everything from diets and support systems to doctors and drugs and I got a closer look at just how powerful this man was. And through it all, his passion and commitment for the things that he loved – his kids, and his music, never wavered. With each knock down, Brad bounced back up higher, stronger, and with even greater belief in the possibilities.

Two years ago, Brad approached me with the goal of wanting to do a triathlon. He knew this was my love and came to me for tips, suggestions, and training advice. I set him up with everything that I thought he needed, including entry into the Avalon Islandman sprint distance triathlon. I was overjoyed at the opportunity of being able to give something back to the guy who, as a band director, had given so much to my own daughters and who had enriched our family's lives with his gifts. My wife and I were at the 2007 Avalon Islandman both as volunteers and as supporters of Brad. We saw him multiple times throughout the race and each time we did, we saw a smile on him from ear to ear. It was yet another example of Brad taking on a challenge and devouring it with the same lust and drive in which he lived his life.

The experience was so positive for him that he came back again to race in 2008, significantly bettering his overall time and placement in the race.

Although a loss like this is painful, we can't lose focus of the brilliant way that Brad Schoener lived every minute of his life. We need to celebrate the legacy that Brad has left behind. Brad touched souls and made people better as a result of knowing him. For that matter, he just flat out made the world a better and brighter place. He accomplished the kind of greatness that most people can only dream of and I feel blessed for having been able to connect with him on multiple levels.

Peace Brad Schoener and thank you.

Post script – Shortly after I originally wrote this piece, I received a very touching email from Brad's wife Jen, which I would also like to share. I am honored to say that since Brad's passing, I have worked closely with Jen in helping to produce a 5K race and music marathon which benefits Brad's favorite charity. I'm helping her build a perfect beast.

Jen's email follows:

Dear Steve,

Brad loved the triathlon so much — he had a "dream page" that he made that he would focus on at night to empower him to

*conquer the cancer. SO MANY of the photos on that page are of
the triathlon... it gave him so much strength mentally and
spiritually as well as physically. I am so grateful to you for all
the support and encouragement you've given Brad over the
years — he always spoke very fondly of you and was ALWAYS
ready for the next race... I remember he was crushed when the
doctor in Mexico told him not to expect to race this year
because he would be too tired.... Brad never planned to stop...
he was looking for a way to work around it!*

Jen Schoener

Leukemia Lessons Learned

The top 10 lessons I have learned during my initial diagnosis, treatment and now remission phases of my leukemia…

1). Blood cancers do not play by any rules. No logical ones anyway.

2). Stuff can happen to anybody. And it's not the "stuff" that measures our character, it's how we react and respond to that "stuff".

3). The internet is full of as much useless information as useful. Talk to doctors and choose your websites and content wisely. Don't just blindly search a disease.

4). Some friends and family will shy away from you not because they don't care; but because they just don't know what to say or do and would rather avoid the situation. It's not personal. It's just their way of coping with someone else's illness.

5). A strong mind and will is an amazing force and should not be underestimated.

6). Support crews are critical.

7). Chemotherapy nurses are among the most special people on the planet.

8). Don't be afraid to ask questions and get second and third opinions.

9). Take things one step at a time.

10). Some incredibly positive things can be done with what might initially seem like very negative news.

The Importance of Being HERE

I would like to recycle some wisdom that came to me from Shep Messing. If you are reading this book in its proper order, you know who he is. If not, I guess you'll have to backtrack and figure it out.

Shep told me that after so many years of playing such a high level of international soccer, he is now content to practice yoga and is happy to just be where his feet are. "Be where your feet are". THAT is such a powerful statement when we think about the importance of living your life in the moment.

I find myself repeating that when things start to get away from me. Often times we get so caught up in the millions of thoughts and plans that race through our minds on a daily basis that we forget about the things that are right in front of us. I find myself also using this mantra while racing and training when things start to feel just a little "off".

Be where your feet are…

The Person Within

Did you ever stop and wonder what sets triathletes apart from other athletes? Or what sets them apart from the rest of society in general for that matter? I think about it all the time. There is something about this sport that fosters an incredible sense of brotherhood and camaraderie unlike any other. Something that is almost viral and infectious in nature.

I'm a little unclear if it's that individuals with particular personality traits are drawn to the sport of triathlon, or if the sport of triathlon does such a great job of promoting that environment that it further defines the individual. Probably a little of both but it makes for a pretty cool community.

I've seen my share of examples of this over the years. I've witnessed guys giving up spare tubes before the start of a race. During one race in particular, a friend of mine missed an iron distance personal record by 3 minutes because he spent 10 minutes helping out a stranger who was struggling with a flat. And they were in the same age group!

Days before a big race, how many times have we seen veteran athletes driving around the bike course in cars explaining each little turn and hill to nervous and apprehensive rookies? And how often have we seen chalk inscribed messages of inspiration along race courses meant to motivate the very same people that we are competing against? These are all examples of things we do without giving any second thought. We help out our brothers. We do whatever we can to help them have a good race and a more memorable and positive experience. Even if that means that their finish time ends up better than our own.

We want everyone in this family to be successful.

When I think about all of the people that I have met as a result of this zany sport, I'm amazed at how prevalent this invisible thread or common link is that bonds us. The international community at large needs to take a few lessons from triathletes.

I have very vivid memories of folks from various discussion forums offering advice, suggestions, and compassion for me as I prepared for my first iron distance race. And some of those same individuals were even more instrumental during race week as they took me under their wing and made sure that I wasn't overlooking anything and that I had screwed by head on right.

These people were essentially strangers to me. We were brought together only by our passion for the sport, but were heavily invested in one another's success. In most cases I couldn't even tell you the names of their spouses or what they did for a living. That never mattered. They were willing to drop what they were doing to help out an iron virgin.

To be able to reflect back on a race and have lasting memories of individuals is icing on top of that finisher's medal or certificate. And a treasure that will last much longer than the finisher's tee shirt! You simply won't find this kind interaction among most athletes in other sports.

So, let's all do our part to keep the good karma alive and regenerating. Let's all lend a helping hand or a shoulder whenever possible. Don't forget to thank the volunteers who are sacrificing their time and energy to help you realize your dreams. Celebrate the fact that you have chosen to surround yourself with an amazingly fine yet rare group of positive individuals.

Take a look around before the start of a race and count your blessings and remind yourself how fortunate you are to have the courage and ambition to even be there.

And lastly, no matter what the outcome is, be proud of your accomplishments for what they mean to you, not how they may stack up against someone else. And should you have a "bad day", make a note, learn a lesson. And move on.

Greatness Personified

On January 18th, I attended a funeral service for the father of a good college buddy. It is no surprise and no act of irony or coincidence that this celebration of life took place on the very day that we also celebrate the birthday of Dr. Martin Luther King Jr.

Edwin "Mr. C." Collins passed peacefully with his family by his side on January 11th. His eldest son Chris and I were good college friends in the early 1980s and have remained so through the years.

Having known Chris for so many years, and having met Mr. and Mrs. C. on so many occasions, I was well aware of just how amazing this couple was…or at least I thought I was aware. Mr. C., along with his wife of 53 years embraced and embodied education. Mr. C. was born and raised in Chester and graduated from Chester High School. He completed his undergraduate studies at Lincoln University in Chester County and Cheyney State College, where he also earned his master's degree.

Mr. C. was the classic example of giving back. Chris spoke often of their work having piloted Swarthmore College's year-round Upward Bound program, for more than 30 years. Mr. C. also taught African American studies at Swarthmore College, was vice principal of Douglas Junior High School, director of the Chester Upland School District summer science camps and was a social studies teacher at Showalter Junior High School in Chester. Like I said, his life WAS education.

I knew all of this simply through my relationship with Chris and from the pride and enthusiasm in which he often spoke of his family. But until yesterday, my comprehension of their greatness was really limited to what I had heard from others.

Yesterday I had the opportunity to witness greatness first hand as I sat in the service and saw the powerful result of the four way intersection between humanity, opportunity, dedication, and love.

I sat amidst men and women of the cloth, doctors, lawyers, and a room full of standup good people. All of whom became who they are today because of the opportunities given to them by Mr. C.

I sat in a room full of living and thriving examples of the passion that was Mr. Collins. I looked around the room and felt both fortunate and blessed to even be seated and a part of his celebration of life.

I realized too that Mr. C.'s character is the stuff that legends and legacies are made of. So, as much as he will be missed, there is no doubt in my mind that the legacy of Ed Collins will be carried on for generations to come. His spirit and his mission will continue to thrive through the countless people whose lives he has touched….and will continue to touch.

I, like many others, left that church in Chester Pennsylvania inspired to do more, and wanting to be more.

An Angel Rises

Given the fact that I am a leukemia survivor, and am quite active with The Leukemia & Lymphoma Society, I find myself making connections all the

time. Connections in the medical field, connections to patients, and their family members, and connections to wonderful people who just want to do their part to make a difference…. to count, and to matter.

I am convinced that I was diagnosed to serve as a conduit or a voice in this capacity. And I love the fact that I can do what I do. I embrace that. It's not a curse or baggage, it's an honor to be able to help others during difficult times.

For four years now it has been very meaningful for me, and I can only hope the connections are meaningful to others as well. I have become friends with some incredible success stories. Real life heroes like Mark Rodgers, Curtis Bronson, Ali Wishnick, and David Wolovitz continue to amaze and inspire me. They are living proof that all of our efforts really do pay off.

I take pride in my "mission" when someone reaches out to me asking if I can throw a lifeline or connect with someone who may have been recently diagnosed. And it was no different when a college buddy asked me to reach out to Caroline. It was over a year ago when Caroline and I first started corresponding. She was diagnosed with leukemia and like most people she had more questions than answers.

Actually Caroline was a little different. She seemed to have direction and a strong conviction that she would not only heal but would rebound stronger than ever. We instantly developed a very upbeat and positive vibe. Caroline was young and had her world in front of her. She had an amazingly supportive family, many of which I had the pleasure of meeting and sharing some of that positive energy and optimism with.

Caroline had hope.

Caroline had options.

Caroline believed.

We spoke often when she was in and out of treatment. I always tried to walk that fine line between being respectful of personal space, while at the same time wanting to keep an eye out and plugged in to make sure things were OK.

Caroline's condition see-sawed over the course of that year. We spoke or emailed when we could and when we couldn't I kept a close watch on her Care Page.

Sadly her condition worsened and we soon relied on updates from the backbone of her universe; her husband, Adam.

Things continued to spiral downward and we lost Caroline on May 8th. I only had the pleasure of knowing Caroline for a very brief period of time. My sadness pales in comparison to the grief that can only be felt when someone loses their child, or their spouse, or sister.

But what I can say is that Caroline Gallagher Cranston touched me…as did her entire family. For that, I thank you all.

Rest assured that Caroline and all that she stood for and fought for will only add fuel for those of us who work diligently and passionately to continue to find better treatment options, and a cure. And hopefully it will do the same for others.

Please don't wait until the time is "better" to do something. Don't look away because you are too busy or can't be bothered to help. Everyone can do something. Everyone can help in some small way.

Do something for all of the Carolines in the world. And one more thing, I believe we have all been asked to hug our dogs.

A Fallen Brother

The sport of triathlon always gets my writing juices flowing. For different reasons, so does the topic of losing a loved one. So I can't quite understand why when those two subjects combine as one that I am practically at a loss for words. Perhaps it's not that I am at a loss for words, maybe I just can't seem to organize any of the words that are colliding in my head into an intelligent thought.

Last summer an athlete lost his life in the swim segment of a local triathlon. Although as athletes we all know the inherent risks of participating in these types of events, hearing news like this is always gut wrenching. And it's even more difficult when it happens at a race that you are involved with on the production side, and when you are friends with the race's organizers and founders. I know how hard they are taking this. I know how diligent they are in the planning, execution, and safety concerns associated with putting on an event such as this. They take each and every detail very seriously…. as they should. But still…. things happen.

But all of that pales in comparison to what Derek Valentino's family went through on race day and the pain and loss they now feel.

Derek was a 40 year old father of two and a first time triathlete. I didn't know Derek, but at the same time, I did. His is a pretty common demographic in the triathlon community.

Derek could have been anyone. But he wasn't just anyone.

He was a dad, and a husband, whose family supported his quest to become a triathlete. While my heart aches for Derek's family, there is a small voice inside me that is telling me that Derek died pursuing a passion, which in some weird way makes it a little better, yet more tragic at the same time.

I will say this to the Valentino family… Derek wanted to be a triathlete. The truth is he already was a triathlete by race morning. The training and preparation that Derek put into this race made him the triathlete that he longed to become.

The Valentino family probably doesn't quite understand just how tight the triathlon community is, but I have a feeling they are about to find out.

We all mourn your loss. And we are all honored that Derek chose to become involved with this sport.

Searching

I think people take on the challenge of endurance events because they love the challenge. They love the idea of pushing themselves, managing their own demons, and that incredible feeling of victory at the finish. (and victory can be defined very differently for every athlete).

I was drawn in to the ironman because it scared me and I couldn't conceive how the human mind, body, and spirit could endure 140.6 miles of racing. The more I didn't understand it, the more I was drawn to it. And eventually I reached the point of magnetism as my coordinates locked on that dream and the rest is history.

A decade ago it was easy to keep the motivation up to train for an ironman (or a marathon for that matter). But as time marches on, and the medals accumulate in a box, that well of motivation seems to become a little more finite than it once was. The races don't become any easier, they sure as heck don't get any shorter, yet training motivation gets tougher; so that's a potentially dangerous combination.

 As much as I remain committed and addicted to the sport of triathlon, I find myself searching for that slightly different flavor of the sport. Years ago, the ironman was considered THE quintessential brass ring of the sport of triathlon. Completing an ironman was the ultimate measure. I don't believe that anymore.

Ironman has become saturated, much the way the marathon became to the running community. And what happened to road racing when the marathon became a little old news and stale? The ultra marathon was born. Runners found a way to push beyond "normalcy" and create new and longer distances. And as the masses catch on to ultra marathoning, I'm sure that bar will again be raised.

Ironman just isn't unique enough anymore. Everyone now has become an "expert" and you can practically pick up a training plan at any local convenience store. So with ironman becoming a little too common place, what's next? What is the next drug of choice for endurance sports junkies? I can hear and feel the underground energy as athletes search for that next …. "thing".

Eventually, endurance athletes reach a point where they feel the need to either go faster or farther.

Adventure racing is gaining a stronger foothold but I still think there is something mystical in the swim/bike/run format that John Collins gave birth to in the late 1970s. I think we will see a surge in more off road triathlons such as the XTERRA series and I even suspect we'll see more iron distance off road triathlons being offered. But for me personally, I have a different answer to that "faster or farther" question.

I see the double ironman and triple ironman becoming the next true measure of mettle. I have had many conversations with double and triple ironman triathletes and race directors and find myself in that same position of being drawn into something because I don't understand it … and am afraid of it.

 Stay tuned.

Laying Life's Bricks

The more seasoned and experienced I get (note – I didn't say "older"), the more I understand the importance of what we leave behind. Although I know I still have many decades of life, love, and laughs in front of me, I recognize that someday there will be a final curtain. And I don't say this with any doom and gloom, I simply want to point out that someday, we will run out of tomorrows, and that should place a greater emphasis on the importance of today.

Lately I have been thinking about whatever legacy I will leave behind. What will my footprint look like? How will my grandchildren talk about me in 50 years? That matters to me. I care about the mark that I am leaving behind me. My signature stamp is important to me. God knows that I have made my share of mistakes, but I have always tried my best to rectify them. And I think I am doing the right things, I'm at least trying. I want people to be able to look back at some of the things that I have done with a certain fondness and hopefully even continue to carry some things forward.

Do I want my kids and grand kids to be runners, cyclists, or triathletes? I want for them whatever they want for themselves. I would love for them to find something that they are passionate about, and devour it. I want them to be able to figure out what pushes their buttons, and go for it. It doesn't really matter what that something is. I hope they find their chocolate. And if they can channel that passion in a way that might benefit others, better still. And yes, I am proud at the thought of someday someone opening a scrapbook or a box of finisher's medals or reading some of the things that I have written and gaining a better understanding of just what all of this meant to me. It's good. It's all very good.

While I don't always know exactly where I am headed, I typically have a pretty sound belief that the direction I am traveling is the "right" direction. I try my best not to leave too much litter and debris along these roads that I travel. (It's also OK to revisit a road travelled years later and perform a little retro clean up. You'd be surprised the difference that can make. Out of sight is not always out of mind.)

Unfortunately there is no magic formula for any of this stuff. Sure there are books and experts of which a small fraction probably adds any legitimate value. Most people find their way simply by *finding their way*. They follow the stars, trying doors and paths along the way and hope they chose correctly. Sometimes they will and sometimes they won't, and that's OK.

How you realign and correct your navigational path is more important than making an initial wrong turn. This is as exact as it gets.

So if there is a message in this (other than my typical fragmented yet therapeutic banter), I think it is that we should all just think about what we are leaving behind.

Are we cultivating gifts of compassion that we hope will be passed down the line? Are we living our lives with dignity and respect for others?

What will others say about us when we leave the party?

Be remembered for the right reasons.

About Stephen Brown

A lifelong athlete growing up in Suburban Philadelphia, Steve ventured into the world of multisport racing in the mid-1980s and never looked back.

Since that time Steve has racked up countless events of all distances including many marathons and ironman triathlons.

Through the years Steve has coached, trained and mentored athletes of all ages from 7 to 70 in various capacities.

In February of 2006, life threw Steve a curve ball when he was diagnosed with leukemia. Wasting no time, he underwent four rounds of chemotherapy. He maintained his baseline fitness level, often running home from his treatments and quickly reached complete remission.

By July of that same year, he was back to racing triathlons. By September of that year, just 7 months after his diagnosis, "RemissionMan" crossed the finish line of his 8th career iron distance triathlon. (2.4-mile swim, 112-mile bike, 26.2-mile run) His diagnosis drew him to the Leukemia and Lymphoma Society's TEAM in TRAINING program where he now also works as an Assistant Triathlon Coach.

Brown has chronicled his journey through remission and across the finish line and in May, 2007 published the book "My New Race" to tell the story.

Brown has also written a collection of multisport short stories, articles, and interviews, entitled "The Inner Triathlete … Forever ablaze". This book is dedicated to Jon "Blazeman" Blais and a portion of the proceeds benefit The Blazeman Foundation's fight against Lou Gehrig's disease.

In December of 2008, Brown released his third book; "50 FIT TIPS". "TIPS" contains 50 fun fitness and motivational tips, reminders, and messages designed to help motivate people and get them moving in the right direction towards better health through fitness.

Steve and his family reside in Philadelphia where he maintains an active racing and training schedule and uses his passion for multisport as a way to give back to many charitable organizations.

Steve also serves on the Board of Directors of the Community YMCA of Eastern Delaware County, is a regional Council Member of USA Triathlon, a contributing writer to HealthFitnessBroadcast.com, and an editor for Liberty Sports Magazine.

To learn more visit www.remissionman.com

About Ethan Zohn

 Ethan Zohn is a former professional soccer player and was the winner of the reality TV show SURVIVOR. (Africa, season three). Zohn used his contest winnings to establish the charitable organization Grassroot Soccer, an organization whose goal is to "mobilize the global soccer community to combat the AIDS epidemic in Africa".

In 2009 Zohn was diagnosed with a rare form of Hodgkin's Lymphoma. After going through an aggressive treatment process, including a stem cell transplant, Zohn eventually reached complete remission.

Along the way he has remained a public and powerful voice in the fight against cancer, as well as many other causes. He is committed to using his energy and resources to make a difference.

To learn more about Ethan visit www.ezohn.com

To learn more about Grassroot Soccer visit
www.grassrootsoccer.org

Ethan Zohn & Steve Brown

Made in the USA
Monee, IL
07 July 2026